JOURNAL

STIL

SPEAK TRUTH IN LOVE

THRIVE IN LIFE

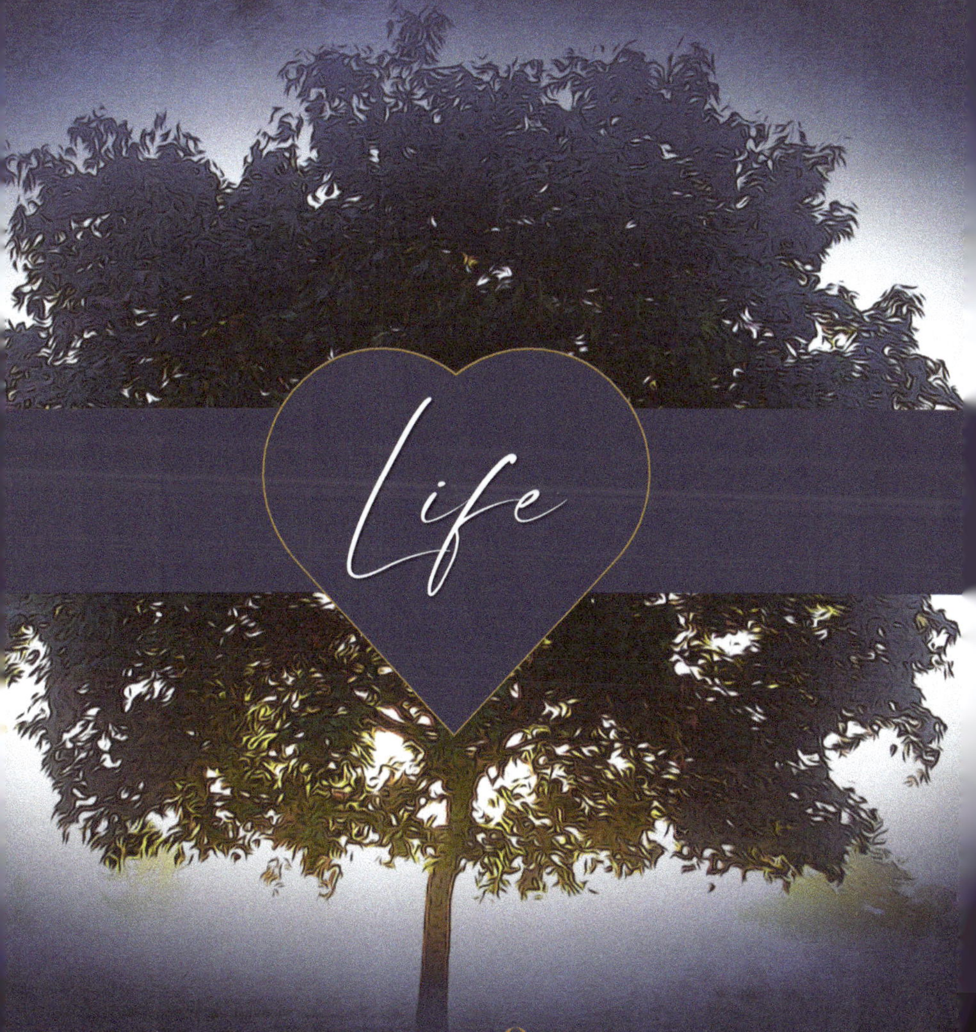

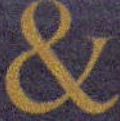

WENDY PIDKAMINY & SARAH HOW

THRIVE IN LIFE

"Instead, we will speak the truth in love,
growing in every way more and more like Christ,
who is the head of his body, the church."

Ephesians 4:15

SpeakTIL.com

DISCLAIMER

Welcome
to
THRIVE IN LIFE
JOURNAL

We are grateful you have chosen this journal to record your dreams, inspired moments, and reflections from the STIL Thrive in Life program. If you haven't already experienced the on-line course or interactive workbook, please visit www.SpeakTIL.com. Our hope is that you will embrace this opportunity to deepen your walk with God, yourself, and others.

OUR WHY

To help you experience inner healing, and a joy-filled, thriving life, by strengthening your connection to God, yourself, and others.

OUR STORY

The Thrive in Life workbook and this journal are a result of much prayer, reflection, lived experience, and many conversations. We are not formally trained Bible scholars, but we both love Jesus.
We are two perfectly imperfect women who are on a daily (at times messy) journey to honor God, love, and accept ourselves, and add value to others.

Thrive in Life is a collection of some of the ways we personally access inner healing and professionally help others find freedom. It is our prayer that you experience a deep sense of God's love as you walk with us on this fantastic adventure to live an abundant life.

Wendy & Sarah

WELCOME

Scan the code below so we can welcome you and you can meet us.

HOW TO CONNECT WITH US

Visit our website www.SpeakTIL.com
Join our email list for upcoming events and updates

Follow us on social media
Facebook: STIL Speak Truth in Love, Inc
Instagram: @speaktil

Schedule a virtual or in person retreat or training

Reach out to us for information or coaching
info@SpeakTIL.com
Wendy@SpeakTIL.com
Sarah@SpeakTIL.com

STIL Speak Truth in Love, Inc.

VISION:

To empower people around the world to connect with God and His Word, and equip them in living a thriving life filled with purpose, hope, peace, and joy.

MISSION:

We provide globally accessible resources, trainings, and coaching that empower and equip people to live a purpose-filled life through a thriving relationship with God, themselves, and others.

CORE VALUES:

Joy, integrity, honesty, collaboration, family, unity, love, audacious generosity, and relationship.

THRIVE IN LIFE

From start to finish, these 7 Core Truths are intended to be built on top of one another, leading you from where you are now to a more profound faith, love, hope, and purpose in life.

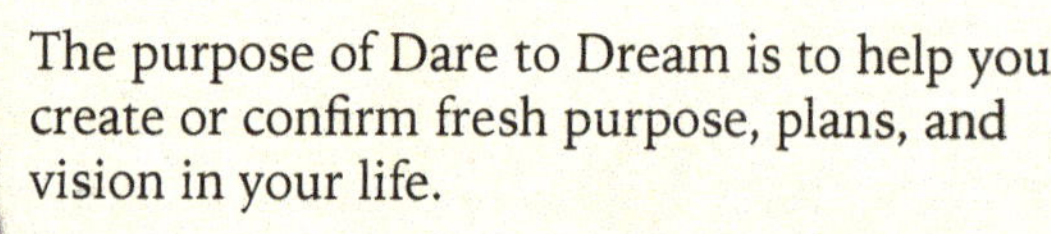

The purpose of Dare to Dream is to help you create or confirm fresh purpose, plans, and vision in your life.

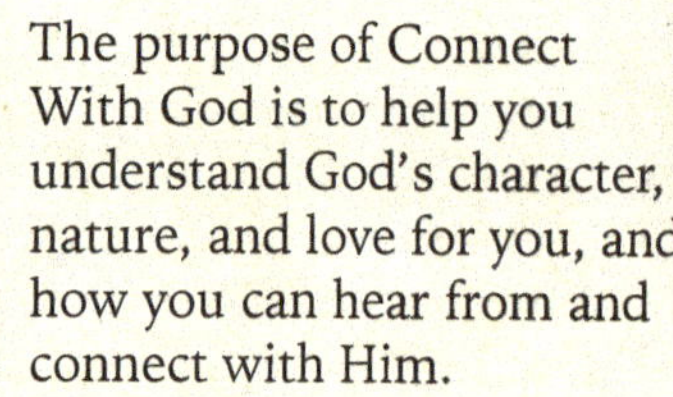

The purpose of Connect With God is to help you understand God's character, nature, and love for you, and how you can hear from and connect with Him.

The purpose of Know Who You Are is to help you recognize and honor your unique skills, talents, and abilities that are God-given and to know who you are in Christ through His gift of salvation.

The purpose of Thrive Inside and Out is to help you live a Spirit-led life by allowing God into deeper levels of your thoughts, actions, feelings, words, behavior, and choices.

The purpose of Come To The Table is to help you recognize, prioritize, and pray for people in your life.

The purpose of Stand Firm is to help you become aware of and apply healthy Biblical boundaries for yourself and others.

The purpose of Live Out Loud is to assist you in formulating God-honoring goals for your daily life and building the future God has planned for you

**"Your word is a lamp to guide my feet
and a light for my path."**
Psalm 119:105

Recognize when you are experiencing a challenging situation, your soul is overwhelmed, and your body is reacting. Walk through all areas of your soul and body to restore your thoughts, emotions, words, and behaviors. Invite God into your areas of need. Embrace God's Word as Him speaking to you. Accept the love God has for you. Trust in the grace, forgiveness, and mercy of Jesus Christ. Seek the counsel and comfort of the Holy Spirit. If you fully surrender to God, He will transform you from the inside out. This is effortless change.

REST *(Matthew 11:28-30)*
Pause and be still. Breathe. Invite God into the situation.
Stay here until you can respond and not react.

What is the situation?

RECOGNIZE *(Psalm 139:23-24)*
Become aware of your **thoughts, emotions, words, and behaviors.** Be kind to yourself in this reflection. Approach yourself and the situation with honesty, compassion, curiosity, courage, grace, and forgiveness.

**What thoughts, emotions, words, and
behaviors are you experiencing?**

RENEW *(Romans 12:2)*
Ask God what you need right now to heal, renew, and transform your **thoughts, emotions, words, and behaviors.** Use the Bible, Prayer, and (if helpful) the Power of STIL.

**What Biblical and practical wisdom is God revealing to you?
What are your choices?**

RESTORE *(Isaiah 40:31)*
Believe, receive, and act on what you have learned from God and His Word.
Honor God while you respect and love yourself and others.

**Now that you have rested, recognized, and renewed,
how do you want to Biblically and practically move forward to
live a more Spirit-led life?**

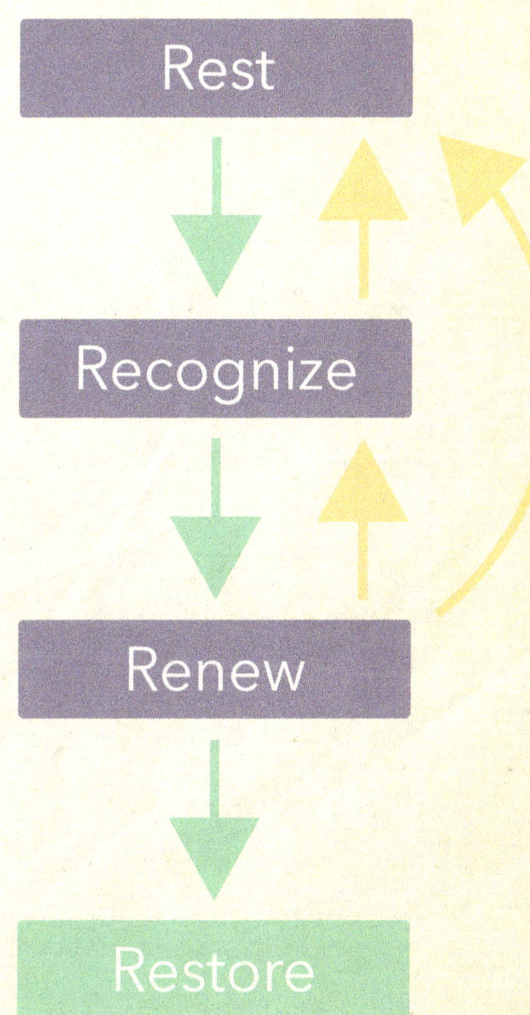

"Each time he said, "My grace is all you need. My power works best in weakness." So now I am glad to boast about my weaknesses, so that the power of Christ can work through me."

2 Corinthians 12:9

"We know how much God loves us, and we have put our trust in his love. God is love, and all who live in love live in God, and God lives in them."
1 John 4:16

What does God say about emotions?

God is the creator of all and called His creation good (*Genesis 1:31*). He created and experiences emotions such as: Grief (*Genesis 6:6*); Jealousy (*Exodus 20:5*); Anger *(Psalm 7:11)*; Laughter (*Psalm 37:13*); Compassion (*Psalm 135:14*); Hate (*Proverbs 6:16*); and Joy (*Zephaniah 3:17*).

God's emotions are consistent with who He is: loving, sinless, reliable, predictable, stable, and they flow from His perfection. Jesus recognized and joined with people's emotions and experiences (*John 4:4-26, 20:24-29*). Together, Jesus and you, can make a way for you to cope, care for your emotions, and make wise decisions. As Jesus is, so are you in the world (*1 John 4:17*).

Jesus showed emotions:

Jesus had compassion.
Matthew 14:14
Jesus expressed anger.
Mark 10:14
Jesus experienced being tired.
John 4:6
Jesus wept.
John 11:35

The Bible addresses emotions:

Joy of the Lord is my strength.
Nehemiah 8:10
A cheerful heart is good medicine.
Proverbs 17:22
Fools vent their anger.
Proverbs 29:11
Don't sin in your anger.
Ephesians 4:26-27

You can choose how you manage emotions

Unhelpful ways to manage emotions:

Avoid
Deny
Shutdown
Act impulsively or reactively
Attack
Blame
Become hopeless
Take a victim role
Others: ________

Helpful ways to manage emotions:

Be curious and compassionate
Identify and name the emotion
Gain awareness
Acknowledge the truth of the emotion
Give yourself time and space
Use self-control
Manage/regulate
Others: ________

Feelings Wheel

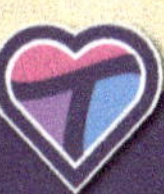

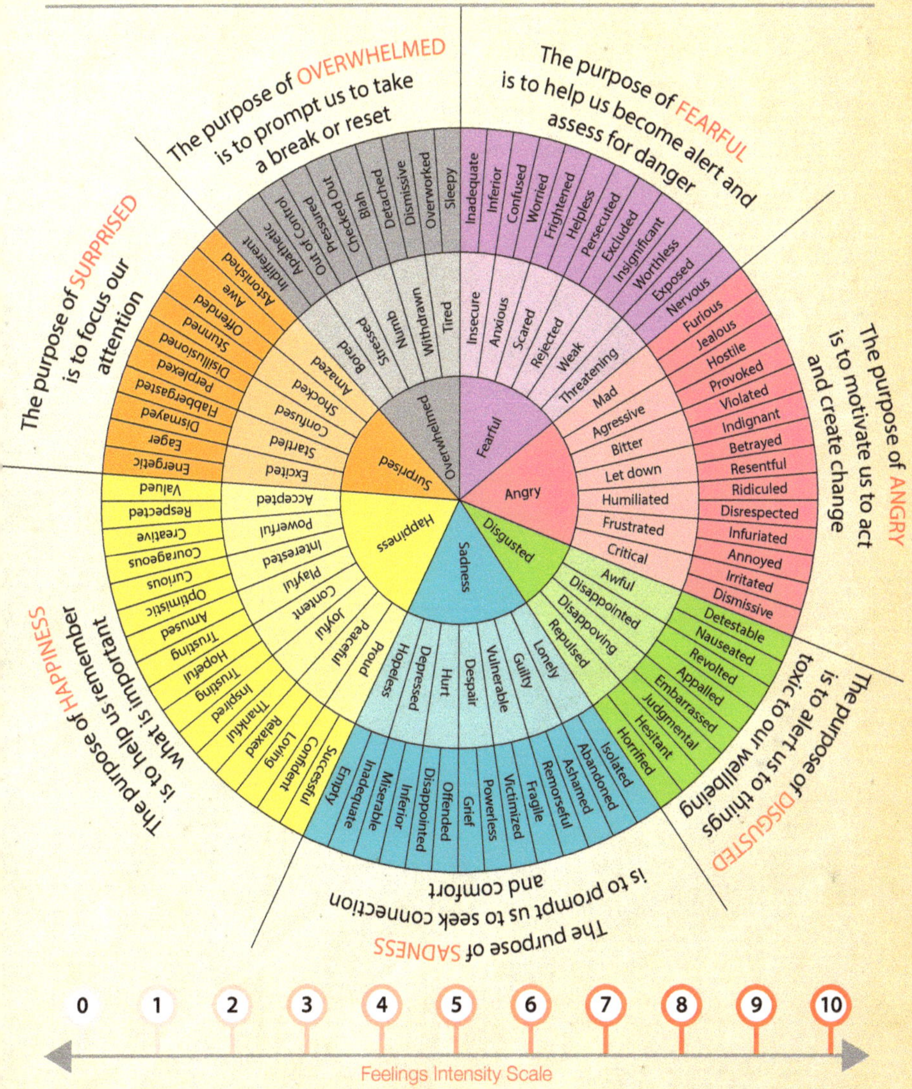

Created By:
STIL Speak Truth In Love, Inc. • www.SpeakTIL.com
Jessica Perusse, LCSW-R • www.cometothetablecounseling.com

JOURNAL

THRIVE IN LIFE

OUR PRAYER

'"The Lord bless you
and keep you;
the Lord make his face shine on you
and be gracious to you;
the Lord turn his face toward you
and give you peace."'
Numbers 6:24-26 (NIV)

Wendy and Sarah